What Left and Right Mean

Clarifying the Political Spectrum

Douglas Giles

Text and cover graphics copyright © 2022

All Rights Reserved. No part of this publication may be reproduced, stored in a retrieval system, or transmitted, in any form or by any means, electronic, mechanical, photocopying, recording, or otherwise, without prior permission of the Publisher.

ISBN: 978-1-7358808-2-2

Insert Philosophy
Italská 209/17
Praha 120 00
Czech Republic
InsertPhilosophyHere.com

Contents

Introduction: Framing the Problem　　　　　　　　　4

Chapter 1: What "Left" and "Right" Mean　　　　　　7

Chapter 2: The Fake Political Dimension　　　　　　16

Chapter 3: The Fake Left and the Reactionary Right　　23

Chapter 4: What Is Conservatism?　　　　　　　　　29

Chapter 5: What Is Liberalism?　　　　　　　　　　35

Introduction: Framing the Problem

Many aspects of politics have been discussed to great lengths by philosophers and nonphilosophers for centuries. Despite this, the political spectrum remains underdiscussed. We are all so used to the terms "left," "right," "liberal," and "conservative" that we hear and use them without a second thought as to their meaning. Politics is complex, and many political conflicts have considerable effects on our lives. We deserve and need a deeper understanding of politics and political action, and we can help accomplish this by being clearer about what the terms "Left" and "Right" signify.

We all have a sense of what "politics" means, and our impressions of anything political tend to include memories of ugly political confrontations. Often, when we think of politics, we think of people shouting at each other and behaving immaturely, which is ironic because what the word "political" really should mean is a sense of community.

The word "political" comes from the ancient Greek word "polis," which simply means "the city." So, polis relates to the political, and all things political are related to all things about the city or society because ancient Greek society centered on the city-state. From the word "polis" we get the idea of politics, the idea of police, and the idea of the suffix of a city in words like "metropolis" and names like "Minneapolis," which means "city of many waters."

Politics is the debate over how government and society should be structured and how social institutions should function and to what ends. The political conflict over these issues is often described in terms of the "Left" versus the "Right," but there is a definite lack of adequate examination of what Left and Right mean. In this book, I want to clarify the meaning of the terms "Left" and "Right" and the left–right political spectrum in a way that helps us better understand political and social conflicts.

The earliest uses of Left and Right in politics did not reflect political philosophies or ideologies. Instead, they indicated support for or opposition to a particular government. "Left" and "Right" as relative terms came from their first uses in the days of the French Revolution. In 1789 in the French National Assembly, supporters of the king chose to group themselves sitting to the right of the assembly president, and opponents of the king sat opposite them on the left. The French newspapers of the time used the terms "the Left" and "the Right" to describe the opposing sides, and the usage spread throughout Europe.

Political groups in the 1790s used "Left" and "Right" to express common ground with one or the other side in the French Revolution. Before long, all political movements opposed to a sitting government were called "the Left," with "the Right" referring to those who supported that government. "Left" and "Right" also became useful terms for degrees of Left and Right beyond an absolute binary. Different political groups could say that they were more left than another group, depending on the strength of their opposition to the current government and the social status quo.

Today, "Left" and "Right" have become such general terms that they are empty of specific meaning beyond a vague sense that Left and Right are opposites. The unreflective use of these terms mischaracterizes most political parties and movements. The corporate news media, whose bread and butter are stories about conflict, portray most of politics as a sports contest. The media opines on who is currently winning the messaging battle between the Left and the Right, with little analysis of actual issues. The portrayal of politics as a spectator sport, exacerbated by social media shout fests, has reduced the idea of the political Left and Right to a simplistic oppositional binary.

The terms "Left" and "leftist" currently lack consistent meanings. The words are adopted by many as shorthand for opposing the rich and powerful. The corporate media, goaded on by certain political factions, equate being leftist with being outcasts; rabble-rousers; or, worse, antisocial miscreants. Left-wing political parties are at best cast as being against the status quo but usually are castigated as dangerous subversives out to dismantle social institutions. What happens when a leftist party wins a majority in government? Out of convenience, the "leftist" label then morphs into the cliché of big government. But the caricatures of bomb-throwing thugs or big government liberals are irrational and calling them both "left wing" is contradictory. Many of those who take on the label "leftist" use it mainly as an expression of opposition to what they see as right wing rather than as an indicator of what ideas they support.

Similarly, the terms "Right" and "right wing" now have a mostly empty meaning. There is a flavor of the words "right wing" that expresses the desire to conserve the status quo. That is what the term "conservative" used to mean beginning with Edmund Burke around the time of the French Revolution. But what the status quo is in any given time and place is relative to circumstances. Do "conservative values" mean something beyond resistance to change? Today, those who self-label as conservative use the term more as a synonym for their feelings of moral superiority over the miscreants on the Left than as an indicator of what ideas they support. An example today is the right wing's adamant "anti-woke" posture, although they have difficulty defining "anti-woke" beyond it being a synonym for "anti-Left." While not presenting a coherent message beyond oppositional politics, the right wing too often opposes a caricature of the left wing that no leftist would recognize.

Do "Left" and "Right" mean something other than "not Right" and "not Left?" Yes, and no, as we shall see. All of the rhetoric from political parties and the media does not tell us what left-wingers and right-wingers actually believe other than that both sides feel their side is correct and the other side is wrong. We especially see this dynamic in the squabbling in the U.S. between the supposedly left-wing Democratic Party and the supposedly right-wing Republican Party. The policy differences between the two parties are much smaller than their rhetoric would have us believe. What differences they have cannot be reduced to the caricatures of big-government liberals versus small-government conservatives, especially because both of those labels are deeply ambiguous and neither party consistently fits into them.

For a term to be useful, it needs to reflect a tangible concept. To call anything "Left," "left wing," or "liberal" has meaning only when and if we know what "left wing" means. The same goes for the terms "Right," "right wing," and "conservative." Rather than mindlessly reuse the same terms over and over, let's insert some philosophy into the left–right divide and try to understand what's going on. By doing so, we can identify the real points of contention between two different visions for society.

Chapter 1: What "Left" and "Right" Mean

Beneath the rhetoric, there is a left–right political spectrum, and political movements and groups can be meaningfully placed along that spectrum. Any such classifications are meaningful only if we have a clear definition of the meanings of "Left" and "Right." Plus, our definitions need to be grounded in readily identifiable social phenomena. To understand what "Left" and "Right" mean, we need to look at some examples of political and social realities and avoid the distortions of political dogmas.

Two Conundrums

To set the stage for exploring the meanings of "Left" and "Right," here are two conundrums of the traditionally defined left–right divide.

The Hitler–Stalin Conundrum

The received dogma in the West is that Communism, including that of Joseph Stalin, is left wing. I remember being taught in grade school that in World War II the right-wing Nazis fought the left-wing Soviets. That depiction is still common. But there is little to nothing to distinguish between the policies and actions of Stalin and Hitler. Both Hitler and Stalin persecuted Jews, quashed dissent, invaded neighboring countries, and ran totalitarian governments that suppressed freedoms. Any suggestion that Stalin and Hitler were in diametrically opposed political systems is completely absurd. Any meaningful conception of the political Left and Right would have to show Hitler and Stalin on the same side of the political spectrum.

The Abortion Conundrum

The received dogma in the United States is that the Right wants less government interference in individuals' lives and the Left wants government to run people's lives. But the abortion debate exposes this rhetoric as false. In its simplest terms, the abortion debate is whether a woman should be legally permitted to or prohibited from terminating a pregnancy. Both sides of the debate seek to establish in law their position on that question. The Right seeks laws that prohibit a woman from having an abortion, and the Left seeks laws establishing a woman's right to an abortion.

This is self-evidently an issue of a woman's freedom to act on her own choice for her own body and life. The right-wing position is that the government *should* interfere in individuals' lives and control women's bodies. The left-wing position is that a woman's freedom to control her own body should be protected from governmental interference. But these are the opposite positions that the received dogma tells us the Left and Right would take. This example is one of many that show that the traditional characterization of the left–right spectrum does not reflect the true conflict between the two sides on tangible issues.

What Are the Concepts Behind Left and Right?

Pulling back the curtain on the political rhetoric, we can start to see what's really going on. One help toward that goal is philosopher Leo Strauss's seminal essay entitled, "What Is Political Philosophy?"[1] Strauss lays down two particularly important ways of looking at what is political. One is that he observes that all political actions aim at either preservation of existing political circumstances or changes to existing political circumstances. As Strauss also very adeptly points out, political activity is dependent on the idea of the good. People who participate in politics, however they are involved, are all guided by a sense of what they believe is the ethical good. That sense of the good is what motivates their political actions. Politics has always been (although especially today) dominated by yelling at and demonizing political opponents. The reality is that people on both sides of the shouting match believe that what they are trying to do is good—ethically good and ethically necessary.

People on both the Left and Right sides of the political spectrum are motivated to political action to realize the good as they see it. Specific Left or Right political actions in any particular time and place would differ according to circumstances. Despite specific differences, we can identify one constant factor among all instances of political actions, a factor consistent with Strauss's view of political actions as motivated by the concept of the good. That factor is power—social, political, and economic power.

The Importance of Power

Over what exactly are the Left and the Right arguing? Well, ultimately, what is any political struggle over? Political struggles are about power—the capacity to produce or prevent change in the existing circumstances. In simple terms, there are two types of power: hard power and soft power. Hard power is the control of land

---

[1] Strauss, Leo. "What Is Political Philosophy?" *The Journal of Politics* 19, no. 3 (1957): 343–368. https://doi.org/10.2307/2126765.

and resources, including money and personnel, and the power to enact policies. Soft power is the capacity to affect social recognition norms and relations and people's perceptions and interests. Hard power and soft power are inextricably intertwined in human society. For example, a marginalized minority group is deprived of both hard and soft (economic and social) power—seldom, if ever, only one or the other. Economic power gives one social power—hard power enables soft power.

The idea of power carries with it some ugly connotations, but not all power is malevolent. One also needs power to be able to do good in the world. Power is needed whether one wants to invade another country or feed the poor. When one has power, one chooses how to use it, and one is ethically responsible for how one uses it. Some people use power to oppress others; some people use power to help others. In all cases, to do anything requires the power to be able to do it, and acquiring, retaining, and using power is central to politics. This is true regardless of how we specifically define power; therefore, the various detailed definitions of power offered by various philosophers are not at issue here. What is at issue is the structure of power relations.

The Importance of Structure

Most people would accept that power is central to politics. Both the Left and the Right claim that their side uses power for good and the other side uses power for bad. Despite this "we are good, they are bad" partisan chestnut, the left–right divide cannot be so simply reduced. The issue is the question of how power is circulated within society. Is power held and wielded by only a few people? Or is power shared among a wide number of people? The structure of power in society is an important aspect of power. It is perhaps the most important aspect of power, and this aspect is at the heart of political conflicts.

The two conundrums mentioned earlier—Hitler and Stalin and abortion—illustrate the central issue of power. There is no fundamental difference between Hitler and Stalin in their use of power, but, more importantly, there is no structural difference in their power. In both the Nazi and the Soviet states, only a very few people, perhaps even only one person, had power. Hitler and Stalin were both autocrats who ruled by fiat. They ruled absolutely over the civil and military sectors of their society. Their decisions were not open to debate or criticism; their hard and soft powers were virtually unchecked.

You could say that Hitler and Stalin were bad people who did bad things with their power. This is only part of the issue. The bigger part is that it was the structure of political power that enabled and protected their use of power to do bad things. The structure of power contributes to consequences. Hitler and Stalin were able to commit evil deeds with their power because the *structure* of the power relations in their society enabled that evil. The political structures of their societies, which they helped to form, gave them absolute authority, and prevented dialogue about any resistance to their actions. For example, someone can desire to kill many Jews, undeniably reprehensible, but only if one has the political power to act on that desire will one be able to commit genocide. The point is the importance of how political power is structured and how widely it is circulated.

Now, let's look at the abortion conundrum that illustrates how power structures affect individual people. The abortion debate is over whether a woman should be legally permitted to or prohibited from terminating her pregnancy. If abortion is legally banned, then all power over abortion rests in the hands of the state, which uses its power to prevent women from freely choosing their course of action. If abortion is legal, then power lies with each individual woman, who is free to make her own choices about her own body. The power structure on abortion could be either concentrated in the state or widely circulated among individuals. Within that difference of the structure of power is the foundation for a tangible, meaningful conception of the left–right political spectrum.

Left and Right Form a Spectrum of Power Concentration

When we combine these thoughts on power and structure illustrated by the two conundrums, what emerges is the presence in societies of greater or lesser concentrations of power. All societies contain social structures that circulate power either broadly or narrowly among their citizens. Power is not a commodity like food or currency; nevertheless, power is something that people exchange and use in their social relations. A totalitarian society is one in which power is concentrated in the hands of a very few, so power is exchanged among and used by only a very few. Particular social institutions or particular laws can also concentrate specific powers in the hands of a few—banning abortion is a clear example. Other examples are legal and social practices of racial or ethnic segregation that concentrate power in the possession of selected groups. Also, structures that perpetuate gross economic inequality concentrate economic, social, and political power in the hands of an elite few.

Here is an especially crucial point: It matters less where exactly power is concentrated than that it *is* concentrated. What matters is the structure of power—how power is or is not shared among members of a social community. It also matters less what the size of the social community is—the fundamentals of power relations are the same regardless of scale. A totalitarian national government, a company town, an anarchic warlord or gang leader, and an oligarchic business syndicate all share the same structure of power concentrated in the hands of a few. A concentration of power necessarily means that other people are excluded from power, have less freedom, and are most likely exploited by those in power.

Human history has been marked by struggles over whether power is to be more concentrated or more widely circulated. I mean this not in terms of simplistic Marxist ideology but in the reality of many different people seeking greater social, economic, and political power for themselves. Throughout history, some people have tried to grab power for themselves and attempted to establish concentrated, exclusive power structures at the expense of others. Other people have attempted to change prevailing political structures, striving to open up the circulation of power to a greater number of people. These rebellious movements have been struggles for both political recognition and material resources. What connects all of these conflicts is that they are ultimately over the circulation versus concentration of power. The particular circumstances were relative to time and place, but they were all conflicts between those who wanted power to be concentrated in fewer people and institutions versus those who wanted power to be shared by more people and institutions.

These struggles over power relations characterize the left-wing/right-wing conflict and the political spectrum. Is power widely circulated or narrowly concentrated? Is a political movement seeking to increase or to restrict the circulation of power? Answering these questions define the Left and the Right and enables us to understand the motives for political actions. Social and political structures that concentrate power into a small number of people or institutions are right-wing structures. Right-wing movements are characterized by their desire and efforts to concentrate power more. In contradistinction, social and political structures that circulate power among a large number of people or institutions are left-wing structures. Left-wing movements are characterized by their desire and efforts to increase the circulation of power.

"Left" and "right" are most informative when they describe someone's intentions as to the general direction of power concentration and circulation. In broad terms, a right-winger is someone who wishes power to be more concentrated and limited to select people, and a left-winger is someone who wishes power to be more widely circulated and thus enjoyed by more people. The goal of the Left is a society open to more people's participation, and the goal of the Right is a more restricted hierarchical society.

The greater a society's social and political structures concentrate power, the more right wing that society is. The more a society circulates power among its citizens, the more to the left it is. Civil rights struggles for legal recognition are leftist because they seek increased equality for oppressed minorities—in other words, greater power for those who are disempowered by the prevailing power structure. Feminism, for example, is leftist in its objective to end power being concentrated in men and change social institutions so that power is more circulated to include women. Conversely, anti-immigrant, antifeminist, or white supremacist movements are right-wing movements that seek a return to more exclusive concentrations of power.

Labeling these movements as "Left" and "Right" is independent of any moral judgments about the people's intentions. All of these groups would see their particular cause as morally just; they are seeking what is in their opinion the ethical good. Sincere, intelligent discussions can be had about whether particular circumstances warrant a greater or lesser concentration of power.

Applying the Power Spectrum

Understanding Left and Right as being on a spectrum of power concentration gives us a clear approach that can be applied to any social situation. This approach empowers us to understand where an individual or group is on the political spectrum by assessing political power structures and people's political opinions, motivations, and actions on the basis of what structure of power they are trying to achieve. Because we are looking at structures of power relations common in all human societies, this approach also allows us to compare political movements in different times and places. Our study of politics becomes more fruitful by focusing on social dynamics more fundamental than particular political positions, which are relative to time and circumstances and often are transitory positions.

Applying the criterion of the concentration of power to whether particular laws and policies are left wing or right wing dissolves many apparent political contradictions. This clarification of what "Left" and "Right" mean answers the Hitler–Stalin conundrum. Both the Nazis and Soviets were right-wing because their power was extremely concentrated in one totalitarian ruler. This clarification also solves the abortion conundrum and other social and economic issues by accepting that the Left and Right choose their positions on the basis of concentrations of power, not on governmental size. Taking away women's power over their bodies and lives and concentrating it in the government is an example of what being right wing is truly about.

Laws restricting free speech, freedom of religion, and so on are supported by the Right and opposed by the Left on the basis of how they change the circulation of power in society. This is why conservatives can support some governmental intrusions into people's lives and not others and leftists can support some restrictions on freedoms and not others.

For example, speech is power, and freedom of speech is a particularly consequential issue in how freely people can speak out against structures of power concentration. The principles of citizens' rights to criticize publicly and to make petition of grievances to the government are inherently leftist principles that tend to be featured more often in more left-wing societies. True, even the most extreme right-wing party can say, with sincere conviction, that they support free speech. That is because the question is not whether speech is allowed but rather *who* should be allowed to have the power of speech. Totalitarian regimes reserve freedom of speech for those loyal to the regime—a concentration of power. Left-wing movements defend free speech rights for those who dissent against the status quo—a broader circulation of power.

Putting aside for the moment that left-wingers are often guilty of the all-too-common double standard as to who is allowed to criticize sitting leaders, the right wing by default seeks to restrict the power of speech to those they deem worthy, whereas the left wing generally seeks to expand free speech rights. This is consistent with the overall intention of the right wing to concentrate power rather than allow it to be widely circulated, which is not to say that freedom of speech is infinite. Leftist John Stuart Mill recognized that a left-wing government could and should, without contradicting its principles, restrict speech that harms others. Restrictions based on Mill's harm principle are expressions of left-wing principles because harmful speech disempowers and silences others and the restrictions seek to increase the circulation of power.

Debunking the Standard Left–Right Spectrum

As used today, the standard left–right political spectrum is based on the alleged dichotomy of the rights of individuals (the Right) versus the force of the government (the Left). It also tends to repeat the myth that the Left is about state control of the economy and the Right is about economic freedom. These portrayals are a right-wing polemic that inaccurately equates the leftist quest to expand the circulation of individual power with statist authoritarianism. It is true that governments have had to intervene to protect the rights of minorities, but to castigate, as the right wing does, these interventions as governmental overreach or even as tyranny is an unabashed declaration that it is wrong to extend rights and power to minorities. Often, the caricatures of small-government conservatives opposing big-government liberals are used to restrict power to a few and preserve structures of inequality.

The question is not the size of the government but the effectiveness of government in facilitating human freedom and prosperity. Unless one takes the extreme opinion that there is no role for government in society, it seems self-evident that government's role is to defend the rights and freedoms of citizens from those who seek to deprive others of them. Who is against the basic concepts of rights and freedom? No one. Nevertheless, some people *are* against granting rights and freedom to particular other people. It is long established that it is a legitimate role of governmental power to protect the powerless from exploitation and abuse and provide for the general welfare. This notion predates any modern conception of "liberalism" and is found in feudal and ancient societies that by today's standards would be considered despotic. For example, the Roman Empire, a society in which power was highly concentrated, still provided governmental relief to its poorest citizens in the form of food aid.

The abortion rights issue shows that it is incorrect to associate the right wing with limitations on state power. There is no greater imposition of state power than a power structure forbidding a human being from controlling his or her own body and future.

Right-wing polemics erect a straw man of the Left as power-hungry statists eager to stamp out individual liberties. This contradicts the fact that left-wing movements, most prominently those favoring civil rights, women's rights, and gay rights, are motivated by the desire to increase individual liberties.

Left-wing polemics erect a straw man of the Right as power-mad tyrants conspiring to torment the masses. Desiring to concentrate power is not necessarily malicious, and it is incorrect to assume the Right is devoid of intelligence or compassion.

The specifics about what freedoms citizens should have involve a large, complex set of questions. We can get past unhelpful polemical rhetoric if we accept that both the left wing and the right wing see liberty as a positive good and if we see the difference between Left and Right in terms of concentration of power.

The power concentration clarification also demythologizes the political spectrum. Notions of a teleological struggle between Left and Right may be romantic, making for good press, but such stories do not reflect the realities of human society. Political conflict is far less about a clash of political ideologies than political theorists and the corporate media portray. We must remember that most people do not live their lives in terms of grand political theory; they seek better lives in terms of economic and social comfort for themselves and those they love. Some people do want power over others, but most people desire only enough power to manage their own affairs successfully. Seeing the left–right spectrum in terms of circulation or concentration of power better reflects how people look at and live their lives.

Understanding Left and Right as the conflict over the circulation or concentration of power puts the question of power where it belongs—as a primary motivation and goal of human political action. Political parties and movements seek political power to enact agendas that either further concentrate or further circulate power in society. Particular political issues are also about either further concentrating or further circulating power in particular circumstances. Who has power and how the use of power affects others are what is at stake in politics.

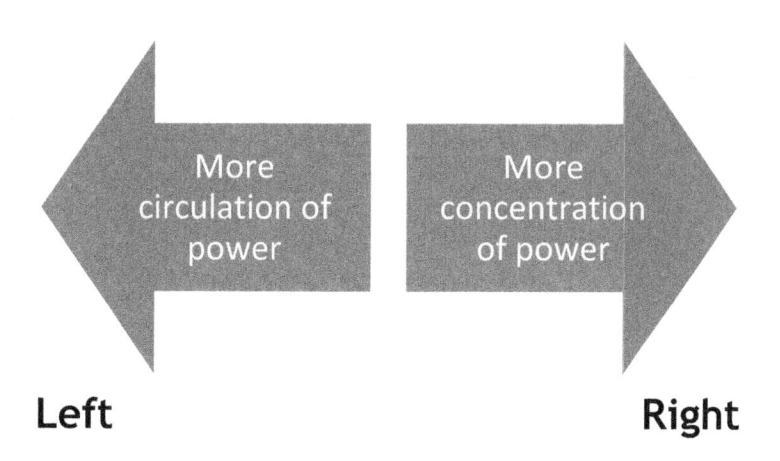

Left ⬅ More circulation of power | More concentration of power ➡ **Right**

Chapter 2: The Fake Political Dimension

The traditional conception of the political spectrum, because it does not adequately consider the conflict over power, has always been inaccurate and therefore confusing. Some have tried to exploit that confusion to push their own agendas, such as the dual-axis political spectrum used by political libertarianism. This marketing fake has fooled some people, and because it egregiously misrepresents power relations it needs to be debunked. In this chapter, I will analyze the political spectrum used to market political libertarianism, which will further clarify the meaning of "Left" and "Right."

The Dual Axis

The dual axis attempts to replace the traditional political spectrum by portraying political attitudes on an XY chart. One axis stands for left–right and the other reflects some other sentiment, most commonly labeled as "authoritarian–libertarian" or "statist-libertarian."

My strong tendency as a philosopher is to acknowledge that issues are usually more multidimensional than currently viewed. The dual-axis chart, however, deliberately obfuscates the discussion of political orientation by creating a false dimension. David Nolan invented the chart in 1969 as a marketing ploy to sell libertarian ideology and the U.S. Libertarian Party that he founded.

Nolan set up a diamond-shaped XY chart with one axis suggesting economic freedom and the other axis suggesting social freedom. He placed political libertarianism at the top as though it were divine grace handed down from heaven—a classic marketing technique to put top and center what you want the observer to prefer. Added are the arrows pointing upward to greater freedom, and who wouldn't want greater freedom? The dual-axis diamond, or Nolan Chart, has been used by libertarian groups and political parties as a recruiting tool.

Image in the public domain.

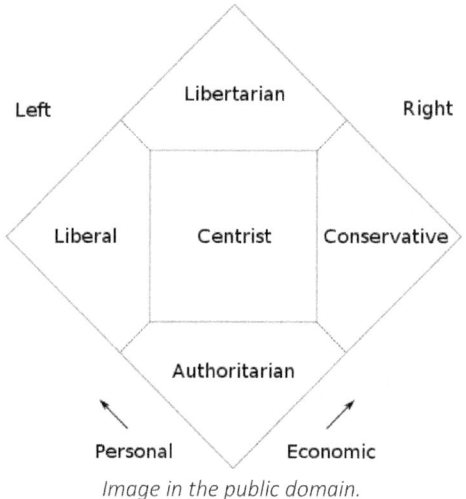

There are multiple problems with the dual-axis chart, the main one being, as mentioned earlier, its creation of a false dimension. As I explained in Chapter 1, the real-life left–right political spectrum reflects the distribution of power in society. Nolan's original chart took that grain of truth and oversimplified it into the bromide of "freedom." Then, he artificially split personal and economic freedom into separate axes to obscure the central truth that the left–right axis *is* the circulation of power versus the concentration of power. There are various versions based on Nolan's original chart, but they are still variations on these two oversimplifications.

The Dual Axis Debunked

The dual-axis political spectrum, however construed, quickly collapses under analysis into the single-axis spectrum of concentration of power. The "authoritarian–libertarian" axis *is* the right–left axis (although "libertarian" means something other than a greater circulation of liberty, as we shall see). The greater concentration of power is the greater concentration of liberty into a smaller number of people. Greater liberty and democratic participation *are* left wing or liberal. Greater authoritarianism *is* right wing or conservative. It is dishonest to offset liberal and conservative as though they are not on the authoritarian–libertarian axis.

Dishonest subterfuge infuses all versions of the libertarian dual-axis chart. The chart is, after all, a marketing ploy. There are three primary areas of subterfuge in the dual axis. One is an artificial separation of economic issues from social issues. This is central to

Nolan's original chart and is often copied by followers. It is an attempt to mask the reality that economic power is inextricably intertwined with social power.

The second subterfuge, which is related to the first, is the dual-axis chart's artificial separation of state power concentrations from nonstate power concentrations. Take, for example, this version:

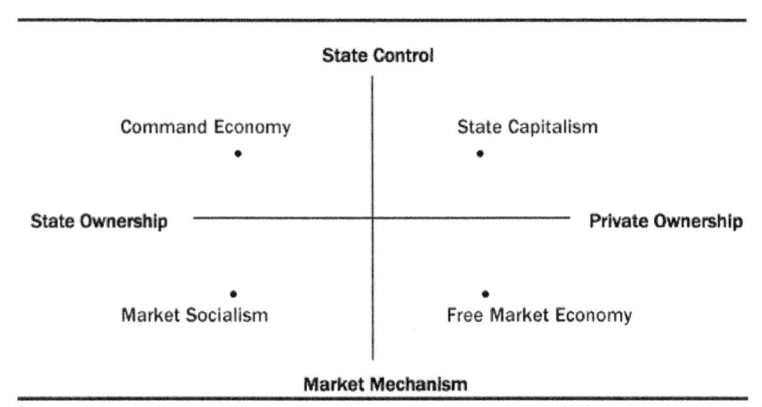

```
                       State Control
                            |
      Command Economy       |      State Capitalism
             •              |             •
                            |
State Ownership ────────────┼──────────── Private Ownership
                            |
             •              |             •
      Market Socialism      |      Free Market Economy
                            |
                     Market Mechanism
```

Sujian Guo and Gary Alex Stradiotto, "The Nature and Direction of Economic Reform in North Korea," February 2007, Political Studies *55(12):754–778.*

This chart takes Nolan's conflation of the economic and the personal one step further. Control and ownership have essentially the same outcome, but in an attempt to discredit the concept of the "state," it splits hairs to portray the "state" as a two-headed evil. Regardless, both "state control" and "state ownership" are the same concentration of power into a single social institution.

The structure of power relations is what matters, not who or what is at the top of the structure. State control or ownership is a concentration of power and is right wing, and so are control or ownership by an individual, an aristocracy, or a corporate oligarchy. It is factually misleading and politically dishonest to portray "private ownership" as a panacea in opposition to "state ownership." Both are subject to concentrations of power; both are subject to greater circulation of power. Likewise, "market mechanism" is not a panacea for "state control." If private ownership is excessively concentrated into a few corporations or individuals, they can and will control market mechanisms.

Whether in a small community or a large nation, concentrations of power function similarly. If a small settlement in a dry area has only one source of water that is privately owned, then that individual also has control over that resource. That private individual can leverage that control and ownership to limit the

Page | 18

personal and economic freedom of others. If a corporation buys all of the water rights in a region, then the corporation can leverage that control and ownership to limit the personal and economic freedom of others. There is no dichotomy between "state ownership" and "private ownership."

The issue is power concentration. An honest chart about economic control or ownership would have one axis—the left–right spectrum as discussed in Chapter 1. The power concentration involves narrowly held control or ownership on one end (right) and broadly held control or ownership on the other (left). Again, structure is what matters, and all power concentrations function and affect society in fundamentally the same way. An autocrat is an autocrat whether using the label of government or business.

Where Libertarianism Is on the Political Spectrum

Why does the libertarian dual-axis chart try to conceal these realities? What exactly are libertarians who use the chart trying to hide? Political libertarians push the false dimension in the dual-axis spectrum as an argument prop to try to differentiate their ideology from more familiar right-wing ideologies. Increasing power concentration is the definition of increasingly right-wing ideology. Again, it does not matter in whom or what the power is concentrated. Libertarians ignore this reality and create the subterfuge that they are outside the left–right spectrum and hide that they are, in fact, right wing. Here is another example of a dual-axis chart:

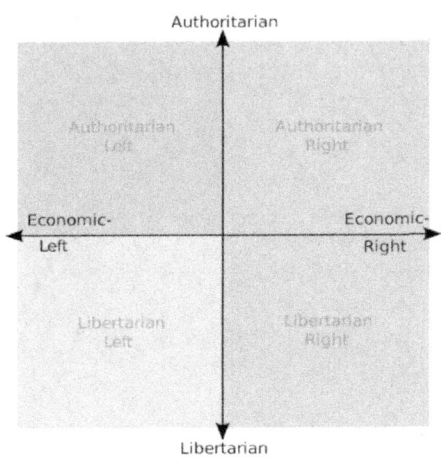

Image in the public domain.

"Authoritarian Left" is a logical contradiction equivalent to calling a shape a "round square." There is an "authoritarian Right," equivalent to calling a shape a "round circle." A totalitarian government, a company town, an anarchic warlord or gang leader, and an oligarchic business syndicate are all examples of the authoritarian Right because they all share the same structure of power concentrated in the hands of the few.

So then, is there a "libertarian Left" as the last dual-axis chart suggests? The perhaps surprising answer is, "no." Greater circulation of power increases personal and economic freedom—that is the definition of left wing. However, the third subterfuge of the libertarian marketing scheme is to portray liberty as an Absolute Good and pretend that libertarianism is aligned with that sacred Good. Not all forms of "liberty" are a greater circulation of freedom. The dictator has the liberty to take away other people's freedoms. Warlords and gang leaders have the liberty to oppress others. They have these liberties because the structure of power concentration leaves these autocrats free from checks and balances that would stop their oppression of others. Political libertarianism's demand for absolute liberty from checks and balances on power inexorably leads to the narrow liberties of the autocrat, as we shall soon see. Libertarianism is inherently right wing in its drive for concentration, not circulation, of "liberty."

Libertarian ideology rests on the mistakes of presuming that governance is violence and governance cannot be other than coercion and oppression. This explains why almost all versions of the dual-axis chart portray government or the state as being a negative to overcome. Nolan's original chart set that tone of declaring "the state" as the worst and libertarianism as the best social structure. Political libertarianism is an extreme opposition to government to bring about a particular form of power concentration.

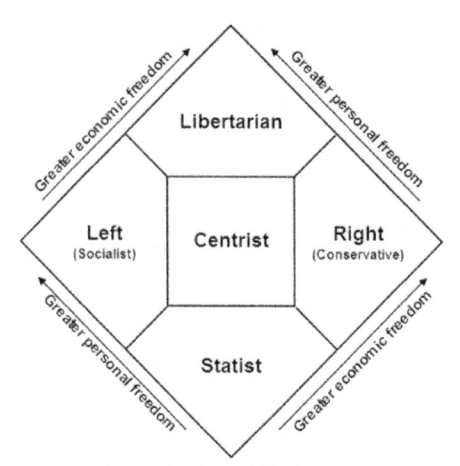

Image in the public domain.

Page | 20

Libertarianism's Right-Wing Fantasy

A central fallacy of libertarianism is the assumption that ending the rule of law—checks and balances on power—would lead to utopia rather than a Hobbesian "state of nature." It is the child's fantasy of "if there were no rules, I could do whatever I want and I would be happy." Who doesn't want more freedom? But libertarians fundamentally misunderstand the nature of freedom. There are positive freedoms—the ability to do things—and negative freedoms—not being subject to coercion. Libertarians do not understand that freedom is a dynamic among people, and they focus on negative freedoms, such as the perceived tyrannies of governance, whether as social norms or legal proscriptions.

Libertarians therefore cannot understand (or willfully ignore) that some restrictions on human behavior are necessary to create more freedom. That is not a paradox. That is the nature of freedom in all aspects of life. Warlords or gang leaders have the liberty to oppress others unless there is a sufficient power to limit their liberty to oppress. Are rules coercion? Sometimes, but rules can, and usually are, in place to bring about greater freedom. Traffic rules allow traffic to flow more freely and safely, and rules only work well if they are obligatory—they cannot be voluntary "if I feel like it." Everyone benefits by not allowing everyone to have the anarchic level of liberty of doing whatever they want without regard to others and shared norms.

Eliminating the state will not lead to more freedom. It can lead only to greater tyranny, as can be easily shown. By falsely proclaiming that governance is violence, the libertarian claims that all sovereignty should lie in the individual. Society, if it even makes sense to call it that in this context, is then a muddle of individuals disconnected from each other and collective action. In this anarchic situation, the libertarian or anarchist, like a totalitarian leader of a state, is devoid of responsibilities and accountability to others and thus is immune from criticism. It is an empty and false view of freedom—a child's fantasy.

In reality, freedom is a dynamic among people; freedom is never not contingent on other people unless you live in a cave far, far away. (And then your freedom is contingent on the forces of nature.) We live in a shared reality, a society in which cooperation and mutual recognition are essential to freedom. Just as a sporting match requires rules and referees to be a successful and pleasurable game, society needs rules and referees to be able to function for the mutual benefits of people. The presence of other people is inherently a restriction on your liberty. Refusing to share the world with other people is refusing them their liberty. Life isn't all about you and what you want.

Libertarianism ignores all of these realities in favor of its "if only there were no rules" fantasy: "If only there were no government, I could do whatever I want, and that's liberty." In this way, political libertarianism is right wing because it would remove all restrictions on the use of power, which would inexorably result in a might-makes-right anarchical concentration of power, both economic and social, in the hands of a few strongmen. Without any social structure to circulate power, the libertarian strongmen would have the liberty to be autocratic oppressors. History shows that even if the majority of people are rationally benevolent, there will always by those who take advantage of opportunities to take away other people's power and oppress them. This is the anarchy of what Hobbes called the "state of nature," which he properly condemned as nasty and brutish. There will always be the active potential for people to abuse power; therefore, libertarianism and anarchism are absurd to pretend that we have no need for social mechanisms to limit abuses of power. The dual-axis scheme attempts to distract from this absurdity by creating a false dimension.

Marketing political libertarianism in terms of the dual-axis spectrum attempts to hide the truth that political libertarianism is an antisocial anarchism that inexorably leads to totalitarianism. That extreme concentration of power of might makes right is what some libertarians want. Libertarian ideology is right wing, and its dual-axis marketing scheme is a fundamentally dishonest subterfuge whose intrinsic falsehoods have tricked some people since it was fabricated in 1969. Libertarians have ever since been creating wacky and overcomplicated versions of the dual-axis chart, each trying to solve the inherent contradictions of the fake axis that David Nolan created. The real solution is to acknowledge the realities that there is one political spectrum defined by power concentration and that political libertarianism is right wing, a fact that the dual axis chart cannot hide.

Chapter 3: The Fake Left and the Reactionary Right

Previously, I touched on how often the use of the terms "Left" and "Right" signal opposition to the other side. This is sensible to a point because there is a real conflict between the Left and the Right over the circulation of power. Again, the Right wants power more concentrated in the hands of a few, and the Left wants more power circulated among more people. Contrasting desires for how society ought to be structured will inescapably lead to conflict.

Quite often, however, feelings of antagonism toward the other side become so strong that the focus on opposition overshadows the positions of one's own side. Overwhelmed with animosity for the other side, people lose touch with the positive values that they supposedly support. These people are not so much Left or Right as they are anti-Right or anti-Left, respectively. These two groups make up most of what people call the "Far Left" and the "Far Right." These often extremist groups are self-defined by negative rather than positive positions, as we shall see.

First, I need to address a common theory about the Far Left and Far Right. That will clear the way to view what the Far Left and Far Right actually are.

Horseshoe Theory

The idea of horseshoe theory is that the political spectrum curves back on itself such that the Far Left and Far Right of the spectrum converge into the same. The claim is that the Far Left and Far Right have far more in common with each other than with the political center.

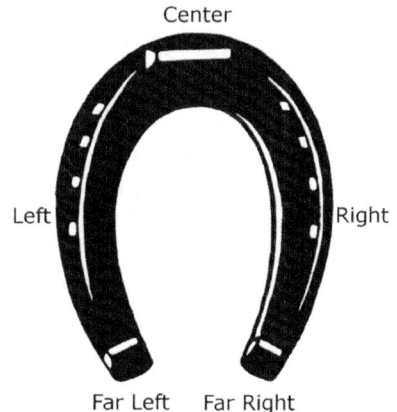

Image in the public domain, author unknown

The theory originated with Jean-Pierre Faye as an attempt to explain how Stalin and Hitler could have agreed to invade and then divide Poland in 1939. Faye created a false dilemma in unreflexively adopting the fiction that Stalin was Far Left. As I pointed out in Chapter 1, there is zero reason to think Stalin was in any way left wing, and understanding the right wing as seeking greater concentrations of power places Stalin and his autocratic regime firmly on the Far Right where it belongs, alongside Hitler's fascism. No need to imagine a horseshoe to explain why they have similar ideologies.

Horseshoe theory is appealing to those who see themselves as centrists. The center can be portrayed as sensible compared to the alternatives on both extremes. The theory has also been appropriated by the right wing to smear the Left as being as bad as the extreme right-wing fascists, if not actually being fascists.

Horseshoe theory ignores several obvious facts. One is that the Far Left and Far Right oppose each other on policies. They have different visions for society and different goals. The Far Right seeks extreme power concentrations, which is exactly what the Far Left is trying to destroy. Their conflict is not the same as two right-wing totalitarians fighting for territorial supremacy like Hitler and Stalin did. Again, understanding Left and Right in terms of power concentration resolves confusions about politics. The Far Left and Far Right share extremism and maybe even tactics, but that does not mean they are nearly the same as horseshoe theory implies.

What Are the Far Left and Far Right?

The simple answer would be to say that they are extremes of the Left and the Right, but that is inadequate. There are individuals and groups who are very strongly left or right, but there are others whose extreme political paradigms and actions are better understood as being outside of the political spectrum. Those groups usually thought of as being Far Left and Far Right are actually neither left nor right. This is because what they have in common is a relative lack of positive values, succumbing as they have to fear of and hatred for those they see as their enemies.

Perhaps it is the case that an appropriate concentration of power would be good for a society, but Far Right groups are not advancing positive solutions. Instead, they are fixated on their antagonism for the supposedly evil leftists. Similarly, greater circulation of and inclusion in power are probably good for society, but Far Left groups are not advancing positive solutions. Instead, they are fixated on their antagonism for the supposedly evil right-wingers.

These extremist individuals and groups will refer to themselves as either "Left" or "Right," but they are more correctly considered to be anti-Right and anti-Left. Because they are characterized by their opposition rather than by positive actions, they are outside of the political spectrum and political discourse. The anti-Right and anti-Left are more interested in taking power away from the other side than in increasing power for anyone. Horseshoe theory tries to reflect the shared oppositional politics in both the Far Left and the Far Right. It is more accurate to think of both groups in terms of their central characteristic—their obsession with opposition.

The Anti-Left Reactionary Right

Those in the Far Right are not actually conservative; they are anti-Left. By definition, the Right, the conservatives, seek to concentrate power in the hands of a few. They act to conserve the power of the dominant sector of society. This inherently excludes certain people, but within the right wing, there is, in general, a respect for the rule of law. There also is, again in general, a tendency toward propriety and order in personal behavior and social structure. Neither of these positive traits of the Right is found in the extremist anti-Left, who have perverted anything positive in the right wing into a hostile reactionism to anything "Left." They hate what they perceive as the Left more than they love values or their own community.

People in the anti-Left are characterized by their reactionary fear of difference. This is a side effect of the right wing's desire for a concentration of power, which can be easily perverted into xenophobia and enmity for others. Animosities toward minorities, nonheteronormative people, immigrants, and women are understandably connected with the right wing in general. To be fair, these reactionary hostilities are more attributable to the anti-Left, whose negative energies have been harnessed and exploited by the more mainstream Right. Major parties that were center–right, such as the U.K. Conservative Party and the U.S. Republican Party, have harnessed the electoral power of the anti-Left reactionary Right but have found their parties all but taken over by extremist reactionary views.

Members of the anti-Left focus more on social issues than on economic issues. Other strongly right-wing groups such as libertarians, anarcho-capitalists, and corporatists seek concentration of power into a select few. The anti-Left, because they are focused more on their opposition to others than on advancing a positive agenda, are fixated more on taking away power from other groups, such as minorities, nonheteronormative people, immigrants, and women. That fixation extends to hostility toward anyone on the Left who acts to circulate more power to those subaltern groups.

A longtime example of this fixation has been the anti-Left's contradictory opposition to abortion rights. If the Right genuinely believed in personal freedom as they claim, they would support a woman's right to control her own body. Instead, driven by their fear of and animosity toward women's power, the anti-Left seeks laws that prohibit a woman from having an abortion. Granted, the right wing in general is patriarchal and tends not to include women in power relations. The reactionary Right's anti-abortion crusade is the position that the government *should* interfere in individuals' lives and control women's bodies.

Adherents of the anti-Left will often portray themselves as fighting in a culture war against the Left. The anti-Left has an intense despair over the present social trend toward increasing diversity and equality. They contrast what they believe to be current social degradation with their image of a previous golden age. Of course, this glorified past was a time when power was concentrated in the dominant class, and many people were shut out from full participation in society. A return to this bygone era of widespread social exclusion is the ultimate goal of the anti-Left.

Because they seek to concentrate power into their own social group to the exclusion of other social groups, the anti-Left is similar to the right wing. However, because their agenda is reactionary—anti-Left more than pro-Right—they are in a sense not within the ordinary right-wing side of the political spectrum. They are reactionaries—emotionally opposed to progress, diversity, and civil discourse about society and power relations.

The Anti-Right Fake Left

Those in the Far Left are not actually liberal but anti-Right. Animosity for others is not restricted to the Far Right, and some people are so full of hatred for the right wing that that opposition is their focus rather than positive action to increase the circulation of power. The Left, by definition, is about increasing the circulation of power, increasing the number of people who are included within society and social institutions, and building community. Those positive traits of the Left are not found in the anti-Right, who, being a mirror image of the anti-Left, have perverted anything positive in the left wing into hostile retaliation to anything "Right." Their hatred of what they perceive as "the Right" outweighs any love for their own community.

The anti-Right is characterized by bitterness toward institutions and people who possess power. The feeling comes from an honest place in that excessive concentrations of power are harmful to society, and, historically, most concentrations of power have come about because of abuse and exploitation of others. Certainly, dismantling unjust power structures is essential to increasing the circulation of power and, by extension, justice. However, the anti-Right is obsessed with the destruction of power and with their opposition to what they perceive as "the Right." They are more interested in taking away power from other groups than in building up power for the people they say they support. They claim to be of the Left but think and behave more like the reactionary Far Right. They are the fake Left.

The fixation with opposition leads the anti-Right into contradictory rather than honest responses to abuses of power. A stunning recent example of this fixation is the fake Left's tacit support for Putin's invasion of Ukraine. The anti-Right claim to be leftists who are against war and against imperialism, but when Putin started a very clearly imperialist war, the fake Left did not oppose it. Instead, because they are so obsessed with selective opposition, they only repeat their animosity toward the U.S. government and their conspiracy theories that almost everything wrong with the world is caused by the United States. They therefore placed the blame for Putin's invasion of Ukraine on the United States rather than on Putin. The authentic Left is about opposing injustices and increasing power for the oppressed everywhere. The fake Left is not, fixated as they are on opposition and, more to the point, opposition only to particular institutions.

Adherents of the fake Left are so blinded by their animosity that they are not within the ordinary left-wing side of the political spectrum. They are so anti-Right that they are closed to progress and diversity, and they do not participate in civil discourse about society and power relations. Like those of the reactionary anti-Left, those of the anti-Right tend to see themselves as involved in a war rather than in politics.

The Anti-Politics of Extremism

Much, much more could be said about the extremists in the two camps of the anti-Left and anti-Right, but I hope I have communicated the basic idea. The main takeaway from this discussion is that rather than seeing extremism as being at the end of the political spectrum, it is more honest and useful to see those extremists as outside of it. Politics is about community, an idea that goes back to the ancient Greeks; again, the word "politics" comes from the Greek word, "polis," meaning the city community. People on the Left or Right can have different opinions but still all be primarily interested in bettering their community—in seeking the ethical good—and are open to dialogue and cooperation. The anti-Left and anti-Right are not. Theirs is an anti-politics—a drive to divide the community by excluding and otherwise harming others.

The problem for politics and for society is that the loudest voices are the most heard. Many people are turned off by politics because the political realm has become dominated by the deafening animosity of the anti-Left and anti-Right. It helps to understand that those fixated on opposition are intruding into and trying to stop the political conversation. The anti-Left and anti-Right are trying to silence other voices and disempower other people. The difficult task for the rest of us is to not let them. We need to continue to try to engage with each other in meaningful conversation.

Chapter 4: What Is Conservatism?

In this chapter, we will take a deep dive into the right wing, also known as "conservatism." The goal is to take the discussion of conservatism out of the realm of polemical partisan discussion and avoid caricature and demagoguery. Conservatism manifests itself in multiple subject areas—fiscal conservatism, religious conservatism, and social conservatism. However, the various expressions of conservative ideologies share a common goal—the restriction of power to a small group, creating a two-tiered society of the haves and have-nots.

It is helpful to understand conservatism as two social groups, differentiated primarily by social status. Because they share the same essential goal of restricting power to a select group, they are both right wing or conservative. Because they have significantly different self-identities, and therefore engage in different political actions, they are distinct social groups. I will refer to the two groups as the "vested conservatives" and the "resentful conservatives" and discuss them in turn.

Vested Conservatives

The vested conservatives (VCs) are people who have a high enough economic and social status that they have a vested interest in maintaining the socioeconomic status quo. For them, the word "conservative" has its literal meaning. They seek to conserve their concentrated social, economic, and political power and their separation from the common people. They are people who attempt to conserve current socioeconomic inequalities because those inequalities benefit them. Their social identity is grounded in a sense of their upper-class superiority to the masses.

VCs include the über-rich and those who believe they are or should be in that upper-upper class. They demand that there be little or no regulation on business, low taxes on the wealthy and corporations, and a government that works for the interests of the wealthy and powerful. In the United States, the VCs seek a return to the laissez-faire America that existed before the Great Society and perhaps before the New Deal or even before the antitrust laws passed from 1890 to 1914. They are the pro-business conservatives, often calling themselves "fiscal conservatives." Their political identity is heavily vested in a vision of government as the entity that defends the property rights of the wealthy.

The VCs are right wing in acting to influence government and the media to promote increased concentration of wealth and economic power in their small segment of society. That is their constitutional right. There is nothing wrong in voting for one's self-interest; that is the heart of democracy. Nor can we blame any VCs for otherwise being politically active to defend and expand their interests. Yes, the rich have the right to express their self-interest politically and have their voices heard, but the rest of us should understand their actions and political positions for what they are: They want to increase power for themselves.

Resentful Conservatives

The resentful conservatives (RCs) also desire the restriction of power in society, but they lack the socioeconomic status and power of the VCs. They possess some social privilege by dint of being the "right" ethnicity, religion, or other social identity, but they nevertheless feel they are oppressed. RCs in the lower economic classes are arguably oppressed—deprived of economic opportunities and power by the VCs. However, rather than adopting a left-wing ethos of increasing the circulation of power, RCs engage in oppositional politics to deprive other people of power. Their actions are dominated by their resentment of other social groups.

Their resentment comes from their dread fear that somewhere, somehow, someone who they want to believe is their inferior is being treated as their equal. Divergence of race and religion are frequent causes of these fears, but whatever the particulars, fear, and a certain level of cowardice about diversity, is at the heart of the RC worldview. Their social and political identity lies in a vision of their social group being superior to all others, and their group must be defended against all who are different from them. Accompanying the fear of difference is the need to relegate those who are different to an inferior status. For example, white supremacists are more than anything else about relegating anyone not white to an inferior social status. Similarly, for evangelical fundamentalist RCs, those of a different religion are not just different—they are inferior to those of one's own religion.

This fear-driven resentment propels the RCs to their fervent desire to maintain a particular homogenized purity in society. Often incorrectly called "populists" (a misapplication of a general term) the RCs' political focus is on reversing the long cultural trend of increasing diversity and inclusion that has circulated more power to more people.

For example, in the United States, the RCs' agenda is a return to an America that never really was, a country where everything was "great" because the privileged status of white evangelicals was unchallenged and unhindered. The RCs believe that something has been lost in the United States, and they blame liberals, especially minorities and foreigners. Theirs is a vision of an imaginary pre-1960s United States of *Father Knows Best*, John Wayne, and *Dragnet*—a world where who was good and who was evil were clearly delineated, and minorities and women knew their place—and if they did not, they were sharply reminded.

In their political actions, the RCs are driven by their oppositional politics. They believe that they and only people like them are the "true" Americans/English/Germans/<insert country here>. They therefore demand that power be concentrated in their social group to the exclusion of all who differ. The RCs trend to be quite politically active, voting against those whom they see as siding with their enemies and supporting candidates who express opposition to their enemies. Like the VCs, the RCs have the right to express their self-interest politically and have their voices heard, but as with the VCs, the rest of us should understand their actions and political positions for what they are.

The anti-Left reactionary Right that I described Chapter 3 are similar to the RCs described here. There are definite overlaps, and I cannot draw a definitive line as to where they can be separated, and perhaps they should not be. Perhaps it is easiest to say that those in the anti-Left reactionary Right are extremist, off-the-charts RCs. However categorized, the RCs are useful tools for the VCs.

The Conservative Alliance

In many countries, the right wing as a political force is a union of the VCs and RCs. The VCs have the money, and the RCs have the numbers, and together they exert political influence. Central to the success of the VCs' agenda is to convince a large enough segment of the population to vote for candidates who will enact it. The enormous amounts of money that go to political campaigns and lobbying of governments are part of a deliberate effort to advance the interests and well-being of the wealthy and powerful VCs. The VCs own and control the corporate media, and they use it to push pro-VC messaging tailored to appeal to the resentments of the RCs. The RCs soak it in, and it shapes their beliefs and spurs them to vote for particular pro-VC political parties and candidates.

It is obvious why the wealthy want to retain a status quo that benefits them, but it takes a certain amount of subterfuge for the VCs to convince the RCs to defend a socioeconomic power structure that is inherently against the RCs' own interests. Money is the tail that wags the electoral dog. Why this subterfuge works is because the VCs can exploit the fundamental psychology of the right-wing mindset.

The Conservative Dualism

Because conservatism is inherently about the concentration of power in a small group, creating a two-tiered society of the haves and have-nots, the conservative mindset easily descends into a reductionist Us-versus-Them view of the world and everyone in it. Again, for both VCs and RCs (although for different reasons), conservatism is the dread fear that somewhere, somehow, someone you think is your inferior is being treated as your equal. From that fear arise the anger and resentment that define resentful conservatism and powers much of right-wing political action. The anger and resentment of the RCs are easily manipulated and exploited by the VCs. The VCs' corporate media stoke the fears of RCs with frenzied visions of imaginary threats from immigrants, welfare queens, gay marriage, affirmative action, labor unions, the fictitious liberal media, liberal politicians, and government agents. The VCs' propagandists know that the xenophobia, racism, sexism, and homophobia that permeate right-wing thinking can be easily pushed into knee-jerk reactionism.

Trumpism and Brexit are only the latest manifestations of a tradition of right-wing fear and resentment that is the natural expression of Us-versus-Them dualism. In the United States, the Ku Klux Klan, the Red Scare of the 1920s, Father Coughlin, Joe McCarthy, Nixon's Southern Strategy, the militia movement, the Christian Coalition, Timothy McVeigh, and the Tea Party movement are all manifestations of a simmering constant in American politics—the anger and resentment RCs feel toward anyone who is not like them. Although the concrete manifestations are slightly different, the core remains the same—a fear of and abiding loathing for anyone who does not fit the "Proper American" paradigm of a white evangelical conservative.

In the United Kingdom, the VCs' Brexit campaign exploited RCs' fears of immigrants and the specter of other nations within the European Union having equal rights with the United Kingdom. The Leave campaign succeeded because the VCs adeptly harnessed RC resentment and right-wing nostalgia for Rule Britannia and its lost empire. The message was simple: "make Britain great again" by separating the Us from the Them, while casting their fellow Europeans in the role of "Them."

Because conservatism is the desire to restrict power to a few, it necessarily sees the majority of other people as the enemy; therefore, making and keeping enemies is not only noble but essential. Such a militantly dualistic paradigm eventually becomes paranoia—the conviction that Them hate Us as much as Us hate Them, and Them is coming to get Us. This is conservatism, and this is their world. And yes, I know that the anti-Right fake Left has the same dualistic resentful mindset—a big part of why it is the *fake* Left.

A conservative is a sociopolitical dualist. The conservative sees the world in simplistic terms—everything is either right or wrong. Conservatives believe their judgments express a transcendent moral and metaphysical reality and that all differing perspectives stem from deep moral and metaphysical wrongness. Acknowledging nuances or ambiguities or compromising with others is a sign of weakness or perversion in the eyes of the strident right-winger. The more fervent the conservative, the narrower becomes the acceptable sphere of correctness. This coalesces with their foundational dualism, making it easy to dismiss uncritically all contrary facts and ideas. What others would call blindness or closed-mindedness, conservatives see as both wise and virtuous.

Thus, within conservatism's dualism, caring about people or the environment is a sign of weakness. Acceptance of cultural diversity is wrong, acceptance of gays and lesbians is wrong, liberal arts curriculum is wrong, as is academic freedom. Right-wing foreign policy is simple—distrust, if not hatred, for those who are different. Any softening of stances against foreign regimes is interpreted as weakness.

Conservative Manipulation

The VCs exploit the RCs' dualistic thinking through fear and hate-mongering. By using the media to flood the minds of RCs with fears, the VCs can more easily convince them to be against laws and regulations that would favor the people over the corporations and their owners. The VCs cloak their agenda in high-sounding ideology and talk of the common good, but their policies are nothing but base self-interest. The myth of American rugged individualism is the centerpiece of the ideological propaganda in the United States. It feeds the RCs' resentment while serving VC interests. Myths are sold under the individualist rubric and packaged in talking points that are eagerly parroted by the VC-owned corporate media.

The VCs oppose regulation of business such as work and product safety laws, environmental laws, and so on saying they would "hurt the corporate bottom line," and they pretend that this would hurt common people. The VCs want the people to believe that requiring big banks and corporations to be ethical somehow hurts them in mainstream America. They push the fiction that raising taxes on rich people to fund essential infrastructure is a threat to a mythical way of life. The VCs claim to be motivated by the common good, but if they were genuinely interested in the common good, they would willingly participate in programs that protect and empower people besides themselves.

There are seemingly endless examples of right-wing efforts to concentrate social, economic, and political power in the hands of the VCs, from taxes to regulations to foreign wars. In all of their efforts, the VCs engage in ideological propaganda that manipulates RC fears. This propaganda is a constant drumbeat in society and influences many by affirming existing resentments and fears. These two groups, VCs and RCs, combine to create and sustain an atmosphere of political hostility in which enemies are created and demagoguery poisons the political atmosphere, resulting in a fierce headwind against any greater circulation of power that would change the status quo.

Chapter 5: What Is Liberalism?

In this chapter, we will take a deep dive into the left wing, commonly called "liberalism." The goal is to take the discussion of liberalism out of the realm of polemical partisan discussion and avoid caricature and demagoguery. The left wing is more diverse than the right wing, so it is even more difficult to define. The task is made much more problematic by what have become two almost opposite uses of the word "liberal," only one of which today is actually of the Left.

The Two "Liberals"

First off, we need to distinguish between two quite different uses of the word "liberal." Both uses originally derived from historical attempts to increase the circulation of power. In their historical contexts, both liberal movements confirm the definition of liberal or left wing that I identified in Chapter 1. Over the centuries, one political trajectory that used "liberal" has strayed far from increasing the circulation of power, and its continued use of "liberal" is mistaken if not deliberately misleading.

The difference between the two uses of the word "liberal" in politics can be partially explained by philosopher Isaiah Berlin's identification of negative and positive liberties.[2]

Negative liberties. These include what we are free from—restrictions and coercive forces like bullying and intimidation.

Positive liberties. These include what we are free to do—having the ability to act on our free will.

Another way to think about these two types is to consider negative liberties as the absence of forces that restrict the options available to you and positive liberties as the abilities to act on available options and effect changes that you want in the world. Berlin showed that negative and positive freedoms can be rival, incompatible interpretations of a political ideal, both interpretations claiming the words "liberty" and "liberal."

One use of "liberal" today is by those who focus on increasing negative freedom, calling for a realm of personal autonomy from which the state is legally excluded. This trajectory of liberalism emerged in the 1600s when the aristocratic class of Europe sought more autonomy from the monarchy, and John Locke's political philosophy was largely an attempt to justify this shift in power

---

[2] Isaiah Berlin, "Two Concepts of Liberty," *Four Essays on Liberty*, (Oxford, England: Oxford University Press, 1969), 118–172.

relations. The aim in this movement was to increase the aristocracy's power by curtailing, even eliminating, the concentration of power in the sovereign monarch. These aristocrats wanted to increase the circulation of power, but only to their class, not to the "lower" classes.

By the late 1900s, this form of liberalism, largely in response to the emergence of corporatism (global capitalism), came to target any government, not just absolute monarchism, as the enemy to be eliminated. Today, this involves using the term "liberal" in its narrow focus on particular negative liberties from "the state." Movements with this view of liberty include economic liberalism, libertarianism, neoliberalism, and anarchism. Despite the use of the term "liberal," these views are based on a straw man interpretation of "the state," and the political agenda does not circulate power widely, as discussed in Chapter 2 about political libertarianism. This view shifts the concentration of power from government to individuals and corporations and is self-centered and exclusionary. People holding to this use of "liberal" are, in reality, of the right wing.

The other use of "liberal" came not from the aristocracy but from other elements of society. These people focused on increasing positive liberties for the majority, not just for the aristocracy. This trajectory encompasses two different approaches. One is a view of liberty most exemplified in Jean-Jacques Rousseau's concept of the greater common good. In this view, positive liberty is what is good for society as a whole, even when that sacrifices the liberty and well-being of some individuals. The other view focuses on positive liberties that cultivate individuals' ability to make their own choices. This view values individual autonomy and sees a role for government and other social institutions in promoting and guaranteeing individual liberties and power.

Increasing Positive Liberties

Without question, the people who use "liberal" to mean increasing positive liberties across all members of society progressively regardless of class are properly liberals or left wing. But that is still a general statement that needs more depth and precision. What does increasing positive freedoms across society entail, and how does one approach this task? Answering these questions will lead us to an understanding of what liberalism is.

Every person's liberty is necessarily limited by the reality that everyone lives within a world. The existence of other objects (you cannot walk through walls), biology and physics (you cannot fly by flapping your limbs), and especially other people who also inhabit the world (you all can't have the same parking space at the same time) restrict your ability to act and thus your freedom to do as you please. In short, reality itself is the biggest restraint on your personal power.

Fundamentally, liberalism means empowering individuals to be able to navigate the inherent difficulties and restrictions of life so that they can live their lives as they choose, free from oppression. Yes, conservatives will use similar language, but they want to empower only their segment of society, not all of society. Liberal actions seek to increase personal power for a broad range of people, not a select group. That means reducing negative liberties—obstacles to freewill actions, definitely—but it also means transforming social structures and institutions to that they are enabling individuals to take advantage of opportunities to increase their positive liberties.

Liberals' overall goal is a society that works for all people, providing equality of opportunity free of discrimination caused by power being concentrated in only a small segment of society. This is about achieving equality of opportunities—not equality of outcomes. Outcomes can never be guaranteed because they depend on multiple factors, including the actions or nonactions of individuals to take advantage of opportunities. The structure of the power relations in society is what enables greater injustice or greater justice. A society that works for all people can do so because it has a structure that empowers all people to act on their free will responsibly. A social structure that empowers people does not magically appear—it must be achieved, and it must be continually sustained.

It Is About Power and the Revolution Will Not Sing Kumbaya

Power is central to politics. Human history has been defined by struggles over whether power is to be more concentrated or more widely circulated. Liberals are on the left side of the political spectrum and are struggling to increase the circulation of power in society. That means fighting the existing unjust power structures.

It is important to realize and accept that increasing power to the people is a struggle. The ideal of a society in which everyone has rights and opportunity is not achieved through wishing it into being or relying in a magic formula. Some wish to believe otherwise, but one cannot just say, "we do this and this and presto, we have social justice!" Reality doesn't work that way, especially social reality.

The harsh reality is that the historical norm is the presence excessive concentrations of power that lead to injustices. This is why some right-wingers believe structural inequalities are natural and not to be changed: it is how things are, and as Edmund Burke argued, how things are is how things should be. Another harsh reality is that liberals have to fight against entrenched power. The structure of the power relations in society usually favors one segment of society at the expense of others, and those structures have existed for a long time. Those who benefit from having excessive power do not willingly give up that excessive power. Right-wingers naturally seek to conserve their existing privileged positions in the power structure, and their power is entrenched in the social structure, so it is relatively easy for them to maintain.

Liberals who want to transform society into structures that benefit more than a select few need to be tougher than those who are maintaining structural inequalities of power. Change is difficult, and successfully increasing the circulation of power comes only after the long struggle and sacrifice of many people committed to changing the structures of society. People into sunshine and unicorns need not apply.

Eyes on the Prize—A Conclusion

Change is slow, but change does come. Political history is the long story of struggles over power relations and structures, and, as Martin Luther King Jr. once said, the arc of the moral universe is long, but it bends toward justice. Every improvement to society has come from the diligent efforts of those who believe in the basic principle of the Left or liberalism—that power should be more widely circulated across society and that all of us should have liberties and opportunities. We owe a lot to the many brave people who have fought for liberal causes and have increased power for more people.

The long and arduous process of struggling for greater circulation of power and freedom is frustrating. The reality that traditional social power structures often create injustices and oppression is angry-making. It's easy, too easy, to give in to emotions of frustration, anger, and desire for vengeance. When people on the Left stray away from focusing on empowering people and instead focus on tearing down others, they move away from being liberals into the oppositional politics of the fake Left as described in Chapter 3.

Another problem for the Left is that liberals are split among many different causes and groups. What all liberal causes share is the goal of increased circulation of power that includes more people in the positive benefits of society. Within this general objective are numerous particular targeted objectives. Different social groups suffer discrimination and exclusion from fully participating in society, and different liberals respond specifically to these different injustices, so liberals tend not to be acting collectively. This is definitely understandable, as resisting concentrations of power and challenging unjust power structures to enact social change is time-consuming and exhausting. Out of necessity, people need to focus on the issues they directly face and may have little time or energy to engage in struggles outside of their personal lives. This keeps the Left divided.

"Keep your eyes on the prize" is great advice both for those tempted to give in to anger and vengeance and for those who are split into small factions. What is the prize? It is a society in which the circulation of power is not restricted to a select few. It is a society that actively ensures that everyone has enough power to manage their own affairs successfully and that no one has undue power over others. That is the ideal, but it is not idealistic. It is how a healthy human society can be and how most people want it to be.

There is no grand historical conflict between Left and Right as transcendent entities. There are many conflicts over power relations between those people who prefer justice and those people who prefer the injustices of power concentrations from which they benefit. Those are the many social conflicts between people on the Left and people on the Right who inhabit many degrees along the broad left–right political spectrum. The world is complicated, but dialogue is the best method of dealing with the complexities of society and power relations. Respecting and listening to other people is the most just thing you can do.

Printed in Great Britain
by Amazon